GERMS UP CLOSE

SARA LEVINE

MILLBROOK PRESS/MINNEAPOLIS

FOR KATY —S.L.

Thank you to Glen C. McGugan Jr., Ph.D., Program Officer, National Institute of Allergy and Infectious Diseases, Parasitology and International Programs Branch, Division of Microbiology and Infectious Diseases, and to Robert A. Levine, MD, Clinical Professor of Laboratory Medicine, Yale School of Medicine, for reviewing this book for accuracy and sharing their insights.

Millbrook Press™
An imprint of Lerner Publishing Group, Inc.
241 First Avenue North
Minneapolis, MN 55401 USA

For reading levels and more information, look up this title at www.lernerbooks.com.

Image credits: Centers for Disease Control and Prevention Public Health Image Library/Alissa Eckert - Medical Illustrator, p. 3; DENNIS KUNKEL MICROSCOPY/SCIENCE PHOTO LIBRARY/Getty Images, p. 4 (top); Kateryna Kon/Shutterstock.com, pp. 4 (bottom), 9, 10 all, 12, 13, 16, 17; Jannicke Wiik-Nielsen/iStock/Getty Images, p. 5 (left); Festa/Shutterstock.com, pp. 5 (right); Callista Images/Image Source/Getty Images, p. 6 (left); STEVE GSCHMEISSNER/SCIENCE PHOTO LIBRARY/Getty Images, p. 6 (right); royaltystockphoto.com/Shutterstock.com, p. 7 (top); James Joel//flickr (CC BY-ND 2.0), p. 7 (bottom); Centers for Disease Control and Prevention Public Health Image Library/Janice Haney Carr, p. 8 (top); Centers for Disease Control and Prevention Public Health Image Library/Jennifer Oosthuizen - Medical Illustrator, p. 8 (bottom); Kateryna Kon/Shutterstock.com, pp. 9, 10 all, 12, 13, 16, 17; Christoph Burgstedt/Shutterstock.com, p. 10 (left); Ed Reschke/Stone/Getty Images, p. 11; Barbol/Shutterstock.com, p. 14 (left); Centers for Disease Control and Prevention Public Health Image Library, p. 14 (right); KATERYNA KON/SCIENCE PHOTO LIBRARY/Getty Images, p. 15 (bottom); Science Photo Library RF/Getty Images, p. 16 (top); koto_feja/Getty Images, p. 18 (left); CAVALLINI JAMES/BSIP/Alamy Stock Photo, p. 18 (right); Stocktrek Images/Getty Images, p. 19; Ralwel/iStockphoto/Getty Images, p. 20 (top); decade3d/Shutterstock.com, p. 20 (bottom); GEMINI PRO STUDIO/Shutterstock.com, p. 21; JUAN GAERTNER/SCIENCE PHOTO LIBRARY/Getty Images, p. 22; Science Photo Library/Alamy Stock Photo, p. 23; Schira/Shutterstock.com, p. 24 (left); Ed Reschke/Getty Images, p. 24 (top right), (Bottom Right), 25 (bottom); Chamaiporn Naprom/Shutterstock.com, p. 25 (top); Laura Westlund/Independent Picture Service, p. 25 (bottom);Juergen Schonnop/Alamy Stock Photo, p. 26; AnnaKostyuk/Shutterstock.com, p. 26 (inset); GoodLifeStudio/Getty Images, p. 27; Davizro Photography/Shutterstock.com, p. 28; Gorodenkoff/Shutterstock.com, p. 29; michaeljung/Shutterstock.com, p. 30. Cover: U.S. Credit: NIAID-RML (top left); Zilinsky/Moment/Getty Images (top right and back); STEVE GSCHMEISSNER/Science Photo Library RF/Getty Images (bottom left); SciePro/Shutterstock.com (bottom right).

Designed by Viet Chu.
Main body text set in Abadi MT Std.
Typeface provided by Monotype Typography.

Library of Congress Cataloging-in-Publication Data

Names: Levine, Sara (Veterinarian), author.
Title: Germs up close / Sara Levine.
Description: Minneapolis : Millbrook Press, [2021] | Includes bibliographical references. | Audience: Ages 5–10 | Audience: Grades 2–3 | Summary: "Have you ever seen a germ up close? Really, really up close? Micrographs and illustrations combine with accessible text to introduce readers to viruses, bacteria, protozoa, and fungi—including COVID-19—that can make people sick"— Provided by publisher.
Identifiers: LCCN 2020021737 (print) | LCCN 2020021738 (ebook) | ISBN 9781728424088 (library binding) | ISBN 9781728424095 (ebook)
Subjects: LCSH: Germ theory of disease—Juvenile literature. | Virus—Juvenile literature. | Bacteria—Juvenile literature.
Classification: LCC RB153 .L48 2021 (print) | LCC RB153 (ebook) | DDC 614.5/7—dc23

LC record available at https://lccn.loc.gov/2020021737
LC ebook record available at https://lccn.loc.gov/2020021738

Manufactured in the United States of America
1-49252-49372-10/6/2020

LOOK OUT! There's something on this page that can make you sick. It's huge, it's brightly colored . . . IT'S A GERM!

In real life, germs are itty-bitty—way too small for you to see even with a magnifying glass. So what exactly are they?

E. coli

bacteria

Germs are tiny things that can live on or inside your body and cause disease. These microscopic monsters are hard to imagine because we can't see them. But with special magnifying equipment and some dye to make their parts show up, we can! Who would have imagined they would be so interesting and beautiful to look at?

protozoa

Four types of germs cause illness: BACTERIA, PROTOZOA, FUNGI, and VIRUSES. Do you want to see what they look like really, really close up?

fungi

virus

BACTERIA

HAVE YOU EVER HAD A CAVITY? An ear infection? Strep throat? If so, bacterial germs were likely to blame.

Bacteria can be found pretty much everywhere: they are the potty germs, the dirt germs, the germs on and inside your body. In fact, you have more bacteria than cells in your body! Alarmed? Don't be. Most types of bacteria aren't bad to have around. The ones that are bad, we call germs.

A mix of bacteria living in the mouth

Salmonella

Spirillum

What do good bacteria do? They have important jobs. Some live in our large intestines where they help us digest and make vitamins from the food we eat. Others occupy our skin like a silent army. They take up space so germs that can make us sick don't have room to move in.

Bacteria are not the smallest germs, but they _are_ small. They are only one cell big. About 31,800 _E. coli_ bacteria would fit on the surface of the period at the end of this sentence. Bodies of bacteria have different shapes, but many are round, hot dog–shaped, or wormlike and squiggly.

BACTERIA

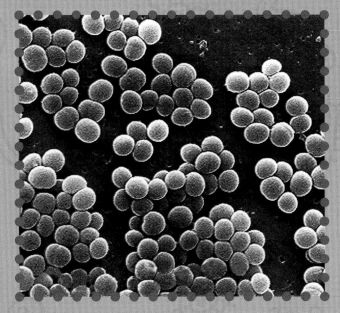

STAPHYLOCOCCUS

HOW TO SAY IT: STA-fuh-luh-KAH-kuhs

OTHER NAMES: Staph

MICROSCOPIC APPEARANCE: Looks like clusters of grapes

HABITAT: Normally lives on your skin

SOME DISEASES IT CAUSES: Skin infections such as boils and cellulitis and also food poisoning

MORE TO KNOW: Staph bacteria are usually helpful. By living on your skin, they keep more dangerous bacteria off your body. But if you get a cut, staph bacteria can get inside your body and cause trouble.

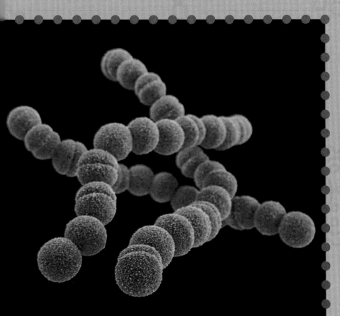

STREPTOCOCCUS

HOW TO SAY IT: STREP-tuh-KAH-kuhs

OTHER NAMES: Strep

MICROSCOPIC APPEARANCE: Looks like chains of tiny balls

HABITAT: Normally lives on your skin, in your mouth, and in your throat

SOME DISEASES IT CAUSES: Strep throat, pneumonia, ear infections, and cavities

MORE TO KNOW: The type of strep bacteria that causes cavities likes to eat sugar. This bacterium turns sugar into acid that makes holes in your teeth. When you brush your teeth, you brush away those strep bacteria and the food they like to eat.

ESCHERICHIA COLI

HOW TO SAY IT: esh-uh-RIK-ee-uh COAL-eye

OTHER NAMES: *E. coli*

MICROSCOPIC APPEARANCE: Looks like mini hot dogs swimming around

HABITAT: Lives in the intestines and poop of healthy people and animals

SOME DISEASES IT CAUSES: Food poisoning and urinary tract infections

MORE TO KNOW: Most types of *E. coli* are harmless, but some types are bad. We cook our meat and wash our veggies to avoid eating dangerous *E. coli* and other bacteria. This is also why it's so important to wash your hands after you use the toilet and before you eat. Bacteria from poop that you can't even see can be on your hands, and eating it can make you sick.

PROTOZOA

EVER WONDER WHY YOU SHOULDN'T DRINK POND WATER?

Or why chlorine is added to town and city drinking water and swimming pools? Some germs that live in water can make us sick, including different types of protozoa.

Protozoa are only one cell big, but they act like tiny animals, eating and moving around and living their lives.

Cryptosporidium

Some are parasites, which means they must live on or inside of a plant, animal, or human to survive. Others live in ponds and rivers.

Like bacteria, protozoa are each only one cell big, but they are larger than bacteria. They come in all kinds of shapes and sizes. Most are completely harmless and fun to look at. Some have special parts that help them move around. Some can change their bodies into different configurations.

Trypanosoma, the germ that causes sleeping sickness

PROTOZOA

PLASMODIUM

HOW TO SAY IT: plaz-MOH-dee-uhm

MICROSCOPIC APPEARANCE: This protozoan parasite changes shape as it goes through different stages of life

HABITAT: Lives in the bodies of female mosquitoes. If an infected mosquito bites you, the protozoa travel to your liver to develop and then go to live inside your red blood cells.

DISEASE IT CAUSES: Malaria

MORE TO KNOW: Symptoms of malaria include fevers, headaches, and nausea. People who get this disease may die. It is spread by certain mosquito species in many parts of the world. To stay safe, people use mosquito netting, insect repellent, and medicine that can treat and prevent malaria.

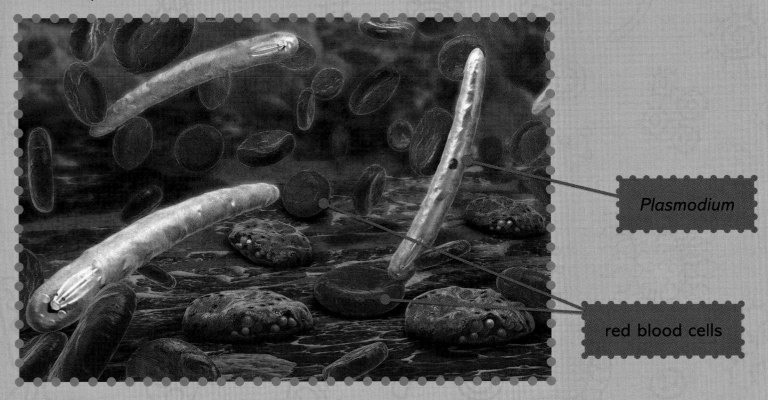

Plasmodium

red blood cells

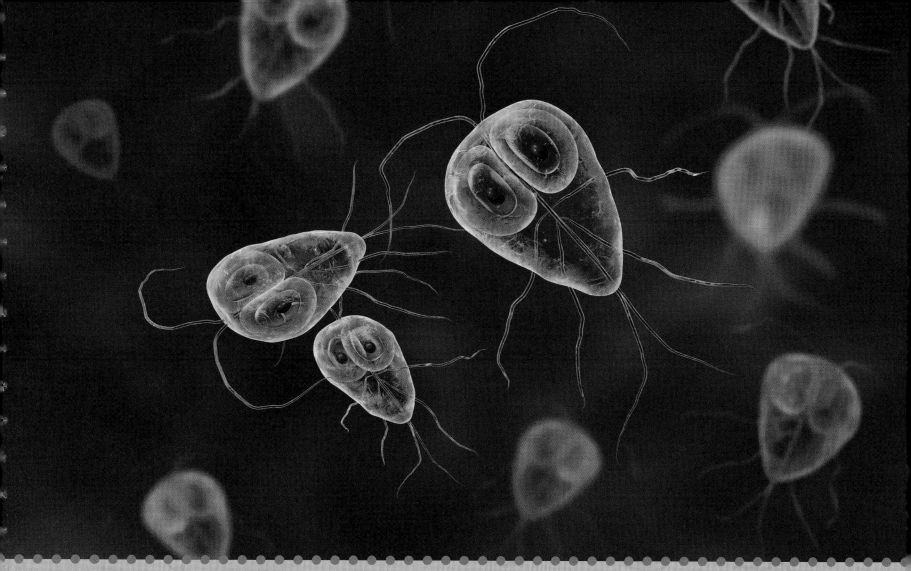

GIARDIA

HOW TO SAY IT: gee-ARE-dee-uh

MICROSCOPIC APPEARANCE: Teardrop-shaped with multiple, tail-like structures called flagella

HABITAT: Lives inside the intestines of infected people and animals. But it can also survive in poop outside of the body, in the water, or on dirt and food.

DISEASE IT CAUSES: Giardiasis

MORE TO KNOW: *Giardia* is a key reason it's important to drink only clean water. People and animals that have it get diarrhea. Then their poop can contaminate water that other people and animals drink.

FUNGI

WHEN YOU WERE A BABY, DID YOU EVER GET DIAPER RASH? Have you ever gotten an annoying, itchy infection between your toes called athlete's foot? Or red, raised circles on your skin that your doctor called ringworm? If so, a fungus was the cause.

Aspergillus

Trichophyton

Did you know some fungi are edible? Mushrooms are fungi. And so is yeast, which helps us make pizza dough and bread.

Fungi live everywhere. Some types of fungi are germs that can make us sick. But other types are helpful, living on our bodies to help keep bad germs off.

Fungi can be as small as one cell big or be made up of many, many cells.

Yeast cells used in baking bread

15

FUNGI

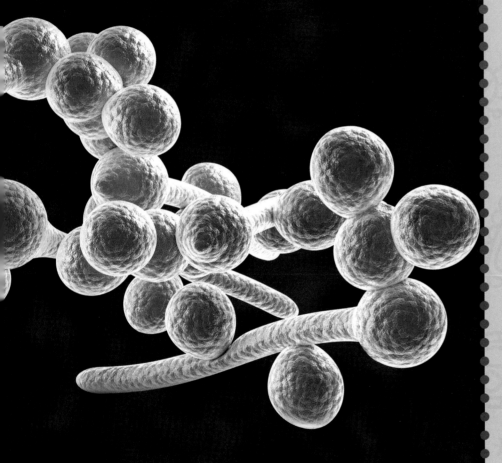

CANDIDA ALBICANS

HOW TO SAY IT: CAN-dih-duh AL-bih-cans

MICROSCOPIC APPEARANCE: Looks like long stems with circles at the end

HABITAT: Lives on humans in moist, warm places such as the mouth and private parts

SOME DISEASES IT CAUSES: Yeast infections. An infection is called thrush when it grows in a person's mouth, and it's called diaper rash when babies get it on their bottoms.

MORE TO KNOW: *Candida* normally lives on your body and doesn't cause any problems. But sometimes it can grow too much and make you sick.

TRICHOPHYTON

HOW TO SAY IT: trick-uh-FIE-tuhn

MICROSCOPIC APPEARANCE: Looks like peas in a pod

HABITAT: Lives on people, on animals, and in the dirt

SOME DISEASES IT CAUSES: Ringworm and athlete's foot

MORE TO KNOW: This fungus has a different name depending on which part of your body it infects. Between the toes, it's called athlete's foot. Ringworm is a misleading name because there's no worm involved. But it *does* cause a circle or ring-shaped itchy area on the skin.

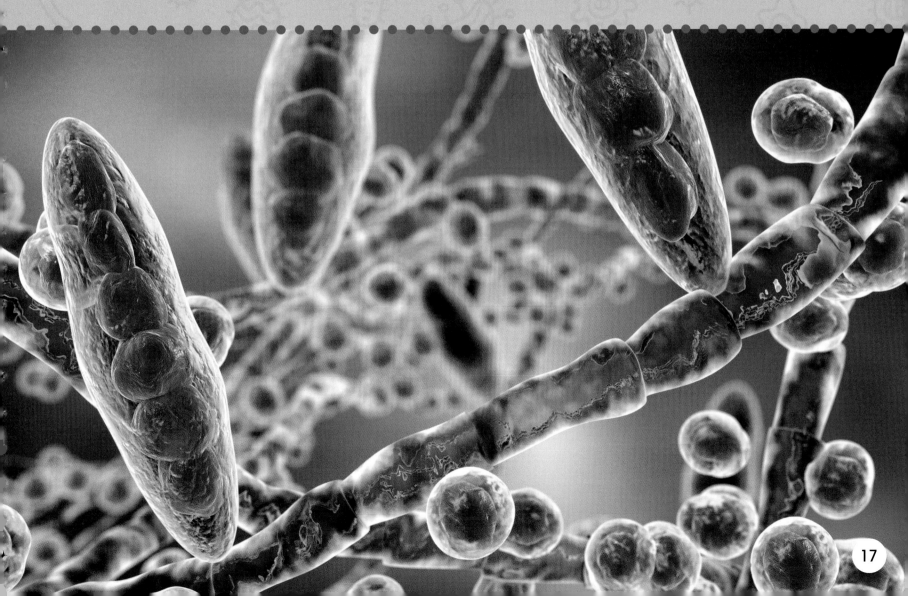

VIRUSES

CHANCES ARE YOU'VE HAD SOME SORT OF VIRUS. Probably a cold. And maybe even the flu. It's also likely you've been vaccinated against viral infections that used to be very common such as mumps, measles, and chickenpox. Some other viruses you may have heard of are rabies, Ebola, and HIV.

Viruses are *so* weird that scientists don't even consider them to be alive. Why? Because they aren't made of cells, and having a cell is a requirement for life.

Virus that causes chickenpox

Virus that causes rabies

Viruses are just tiny bundles of instructions, called DNA or RNA, wrapped in a coat of protein. They can't exist for very long outside of a cell. But when they find a cell to inhabit, they act as if they're alive. They can go inside the cell and take it over, using the cell's reproductive machinery to make more viruses.

Viruses are very tiny, so small you can't see them under a regular microscope. They are much smaller than all the other types of germs. They come in many different shapes.

VIRUSES

INFLUENZA

HOW TO SAY IT: in-flew-EN-zuh

MICROSCOPIC APPEARANCE: Looks like a sphere covered with knobs

HABITAT: Lives inside the nose, throat, and airways of people who are infected

DISEASE IT CAUSES: Flu

MORE TO KNOW: Signs of the flu include coughing, sneezing, sore throat, aches, and pains. It spreads from person to person in tiny water droplets that move through the air when someone coughs, sneezes, or talks. This virus is a tricky one to prevent because it changes shape a lot. This is why people need to get a new, slightly different, flu vaccination every year.

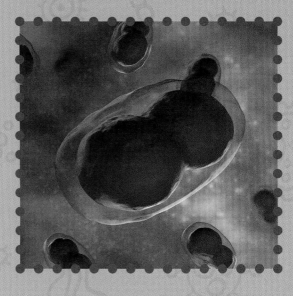

VARIOLA VIRUS

HOW TO SAY IT: vah-ree-OH-luh VIE-ruhs

MICROSCOPIC APPEARANCE: Looks like an oval with a dumbbell shape in the middle

HABITAT: Was in humans, but not anymore. Now lives only in laboratories.

DISEASE IT CAUSES: Smallpox

MORE TO KNOW: This virus used to be a common cause of death, but it was stopped worldwide by the creation and use of a vaccine. The last naturally occurring case was in 1977.

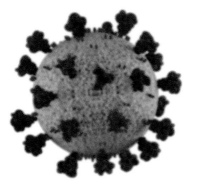

CORONAVIRUS

HOW TO SAY IT: kuh-ROW-nuh-VIE-ruhs

MICROSCOPIC APPEARANCE: Looks like a sphere with crownlike spikes

HABITAT: Lives inside the cells of humans and some animals

SOME DISEASES IT CAUSES: SARS, COVID-19, and some common colds

MORE TO KNOW: There are many types of coronaviruses. One called SARS-CoV-2 (SARZ-coh-VEE-too) started the global pandemic of COVID-19 in 2019. Symptoms of this disease include fever, coughing, difficulty breathing, and losing one's sense of taste and smell. Scientists around the world are working to create a vaccine that will protect us from this virus.

WHEN GERMS GET IN

Bacteria on a pore in the skin

SO GERMS MIGHT BE ENTERTAINING TO LEARN ABOUT OR PRETTY TO LOOK AT, BUT WE DON'T WANT THEM TO MAKE OUR BODIES THEIR NEW HOMES. How do you keep them far away? And how can you fight them when they get inside of you?

The good news is that our bodies take care of most of this for us. We come with a built-in system to keep out and fight off germs. It's called the immune system.

Our skin is a big way we stay protected from germs—it keeps lots of them from ever getting inside. We have a lining over our eyes, in our mouths and noses, and in other body openings that works the same way. However, germs can enter our bodies through cuts or holes. They might get in when you rub your eyes, pick your nose, fall down and scrape your knee, or wiggle a loose tooth. Where we have openings to the outside, we do have saliva and mucus to help kill germs and keep them from getting farther inside. What if a germ makes it into the mouth and down to the stomach? Don't worry—acid in your stomach will kill most any germ.

Cross-section of skin up close

Inside us we also have an army of cells called white blood cells that fight off germs. Different kinds of white blood cells have different jobs. Some kill germs by eating them.

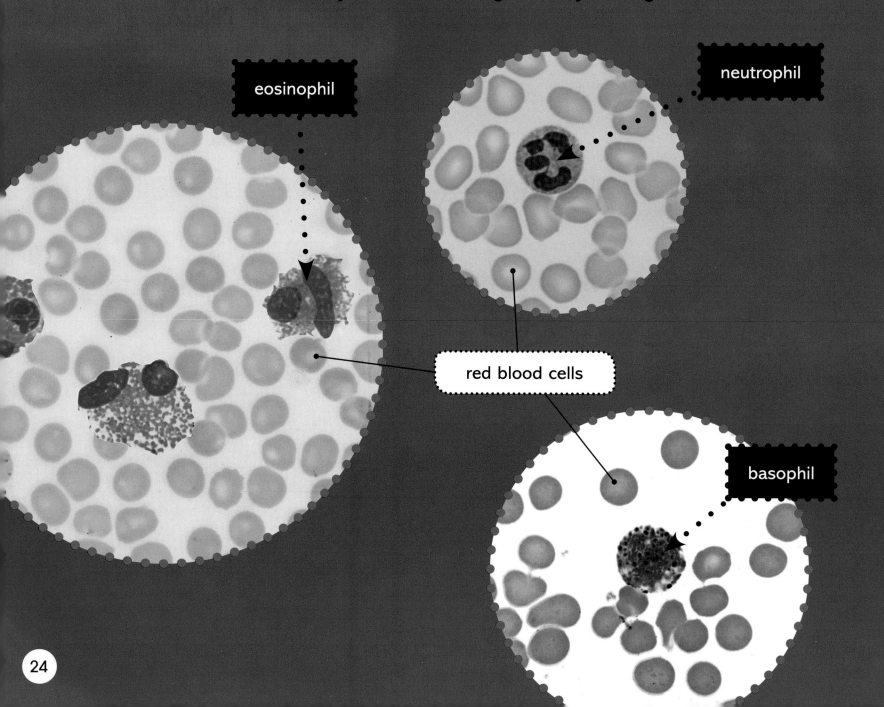

eosinophil

neutrophil

red blood cells

basophil

Some kill them by poking holes in them. Some recognize germs they've encountered before and mark them for destruction.

red blood cell

monocyte

lymphocyte

These photos compare the shapes and sizes of different types of white blood cells.

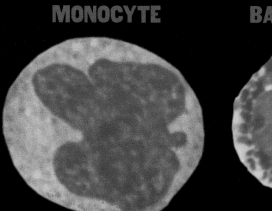

MONOCYTE

BASOPHIL

EOSINOPHIL

NEUTROPHIL

LYMPHOCYTE

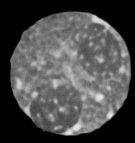
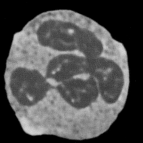

But what about those few germs that get inside and aren't killed right away?

How can we protect ourselves from those germs?

We can wash our hands, especially after using the toilet and before eating. Soap and water are the best way to keep germs away.

We can cough into our elbows rather than our hands. That way we don't get germs on our hands that we might accidentally spread to other people or objects others might touch.

We can wear masks to prevent the spread of germs that travel through the air.

We can cook our food well to kill any germs on it. And we can drink only clean water.

We can also get vaccines to help prevent some diseases, especially those caused by viruses.

A vaccine works by introducing a fake germ into the body, one that won't really make a person sick. The fake germ is either part of a real one or a dead one—the important thing is that it has the same shape as the real germ. The white blood cells in charge of learning to fight off germs will come fight off the fake germ.

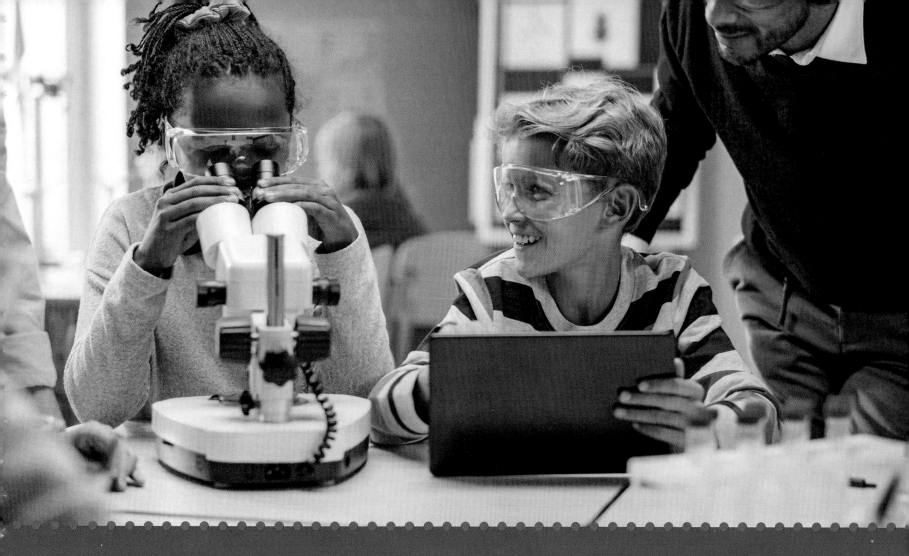

Then if the real germ comes inside the body, those white blood cells will already know how to attack germs with this particular shape. They will be prepared.

Vaccines not only keep you safe by preventing you from getting a disease, but they also help everyone else by not giving viruses a place to live and grow and spread.

If you do get sick from a germ, sometimes there's a medicine you can take to help you get better. Antibiotics kill bacteria. Antivirals destroy some viruses or keep them from reproducing. Other types of medicine can be used to kill fungi and protozoa.

You might think germs are cool. Or you might think they're scary. Either way, learning about them is one more way you can stay healthy.

A doctor can help you get better by prescribing medicine to fight germs.

GLOSSARY

acid: a liquid with certain characteristics including being sour and so strong it can dissolve some metals

bacteria: a group of living things with certain characteristics including being one cell big and lacking a nucleus. Some are considered to be germs.

boil: a painful, red, swollen bump under the skin with pus inside

cell: the smallest unit with the basic properties of life. Some living things are made up of just one cell and others are made up of many.

cellulitis: a painful, red, swollen area on the skin caused by a bacterial infection

digest: break down food into smaller pieces so it can be used in the body

DNA: is short for deoxyribonucleic acid. It is the material inside a cell that carries instructions for how a living thing should look and function.

dye: a substance (also called a stain) added to change the color of something, such as a cell or a germ to make it show up more clearly

fungi: a group of living things with certain characteristics including needing to eat food and digesting their food outside their bodies. Some are considered to be germs.

HIV: is short for human immunodeficiency virus. This virus attacks a type of white blood cell and is the virus that causes AIDS.

immune system: the parts of the body that work together to fight off disease

infection: a disease caused by germs

microscope: an instrument with lenses used to make small things appear larger

microscopic: very small. So small you need a microscope to see it.

nucleus: a part present in most types of cells that holds the DNA and is in charge of how the cell works

pandemic: a disease that quickly spreads to a lot of people in many countries all over the world

parasite: a living thing that lives on or inside the body of another living thing and gets its food or shelter from its host

pneumonia: a lung infection

protozoa: a group of living things with certain characteristics such as being one cell big and having a nucleus. Some are considered to be germs.

pus: the white liquid that forms when there is an infection, made of white blood cells, bacteria, and dead cells

RNA: is short for ribonucleic acid. It is a material inside cells with instructions for making proteins.

vaccine: a substance that is put into a body, usually through a shot, that teaches the body how to fight off a germ and prevent infection

virus: a very tiny germ that is not made of a cell and must be inside a living thing to grow and reproduce

white blood cell: a type of cell that fights off infections in the body

GERMY JOBS

Are you really interested in germs? Here are some careers to consider if you want to find out more about germs or help sick people or animals:

epidemiologist: a scientist who studies how diseases affect the health of groups of people and how to control the spread of these diseases

immunologist: a scientist who studies the immune system or a doctor who treats things that can go wrong with it

infectious disease expert: a scientist who studies diseases caused by germs or a doctor who treats diseases caused by germs

microbiologist: a scientist who studies germs

mycologist: a scientist who studies fungi

nurse: a person with special training who takes care of people who are sick or injured

parasitologist: a scientist who studies parasites

pharmacologist: a scientist who figures out how to make medicines to kill germs and cure diseases

physician: a doctor who figures out what is making people sick and how to make them better

veterinarian: a doctor who figures out what is making animals sick and how to make them better

virologist: a scientist who studies viruses

LEARN MORE

Ben-Barak, Idan. *Do Not Lick This Book*: *It's Full of Germs.* New York: Roaring Brook, 2018.

Davies, Nicola. *Tiny Creatures: The World of Microbes.* Somerville, MA: Candlewick, 2014.

Germs: Bacteria, Viruses, Fungi, and Protozoa. https://kidshealth.org/en/parents/germs.html

"The Island of Explained": *Today, Explained* https://podcasts.apple.com/us/podcast/today-explained/id1346207297?i=1000473290123

Lindeen, Mary. *Stay Healthy with Sesame Street: Understanding Coronavirus.* Minneapolis: Lerner Publications, 2021.

Wicks, Maris. *Human Body Theater.* New York: First Second, 2015.